Mr. Popper's Penguins

Written by
Richard & Florence Atwater

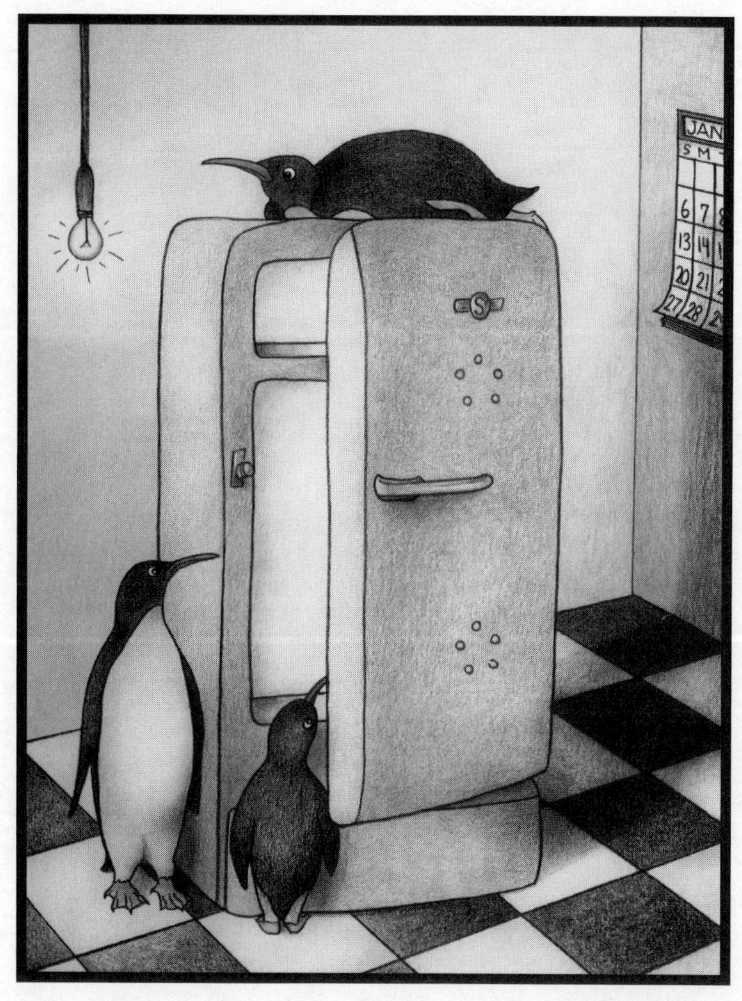

Student Guide

Leigh Lowe

MEMORIA PRESS
www.MemoriaPress.com

MR. POPPER'S PENGUINS
Written by Richard & Florence Atwater

STUDENT GUIDE
Leigh Lowe

ISBN 978-1-61538-034-3

Cover illustration by Starr Steinbach

Mr. Popper's Penguins

PREPARING TO READ:

REVIEW

- Orally review any previous vocabulary.
- Review the plot of the book as read so far.
- Periodically review the concepts of character, setting, and plot.

STUDY GUIDE PREVIEW

- Pronounce & Spell
  - Read aloud together so that students will recognize words when they come across them in their reading. Talk about any words students don't know the meanings of.
- Vocabulary:
  - Read through the vocabulary section of the study guide with students so they are prepared to look for these words as they read.

READING:

- Student reads the chapter (or selection of the chapter for that lesson) independently or to the teacher (for younger students).
- For younger students, you can alternate between teacher-read and student-read passages. Model good reading skills. Encourage students to read expressively and smoothly. Teacher may occasionally take oral reading grades.
- While reading, mark each vocabulary word as you come across it.
- Have students take note in their study guide margin of pages where a comprehension question is answered.

AFTER READING:

VOCABULARY

- Look at each word within the context that it is used, and help your student come up with the best synonym that defines the word. (Make sure it is a synonym the student knows the meaning of.)
- Record the word's meaning in the students' study guides. (Use students' knowledge of Latin and other vocabulary to decipher meanings.)

COMPREHENSION QUESTIONS

- Older students can answer these questions independently, but younger students (2nd-4th) need to answer the questions orally, form a good sentence, and then write it down, using correct punctuation, capitalization, and spelling. (You may want to write the sentence down for the younger student after forming it orally, and then let the student copy it perfectly.)
- It is not necessary to write the answer to every question. Some may be better answered orally.
- Answering questions and composing answers is a valuable learning activity. Questions require students to think; writing a concise answer is a good composition exercise.

ENRICHMENT

- The Enrichment activities include composition, copywork, dictation, research, mapping, drawing, poetry work, literary terms, and more.
- This section has a variety of activities in it, but the most valuable activity is composition. Your student should complete at least one composition assignment each week. Proof student's work and have student copy composition until grammatically perfect. Insist on clear, concise writing. For younger students, start with 2-3 sentences, and do the assignment together. The student can form good sentences orally as you write them down, and then the student copies them.
- These activities can be completed as time and interest allow. Do not feel you need to complete all of these activities. Choose the ones that you feel are the best use of your students' time.

Pronounce & Spell

Himalayas	Antarctic	scientist	Arctic
South Sea	Poles	regions	India

Vocabulary

Write the meaning of each bold word or phrase.

1. He was spattered here and there with paint and **calcimine** ______________________________

   ____

2. he was rather an **untidy** man. ______________________________

   ____

3. Mr. Popper was so **absent-minded** … always dreaming about far-away countries. _______

   ____

4. He had never seen those great shining white **expanses** of ice and snow. ______________

   ____

5. he might have joined some of the great Polar **expeditions**. ______________________________

   ____

6. When he came to the gate of the neat little **bungalow** ______________________________

   ____

7. I have saved a little, and I **daresay** we can get along as we have other winters. __________

   ____

Comprehension Questions

1. Describe Mr. Popper. ______

2. What is Mr. Popper's occupation? ______

3. What does Mr. Popper dream about most? ______

4. Why are evenings the best time of all for Mr Popper? ______

5. Why is Mr. Popper happy it is the end of September? ______

6. What is Mrs. Popper worried about? ______

Activity

Complete the following:

- Draw a picture of the Popper Family. Use details from the book.
- Find the locations Mr. Popper dreamed about on a map. Guess why each might appeal to him.
- Think of an exotic place you would like to visit. Explain your choice.
- Write five sentences that describe Mr. Popper and his family. Use details from the book and choose your own strong adjectives.

Pronounce & Spell

quiet	interrupt	admitted	except
twenty-ninth	gracious	commanded	stomachs

Vocabulary

Write the meaning of each bold word or phrase.

1. As he put on his **spectacles**, he was quite pleased at the prospect ____________________

____

2. answered Mrs. Popper, a little **sharply**. ____________________

____

3. She was not at all a disagreeable woman, but she sometimes got rather **cross** __________

____

4. They sound to me like pretty **heathen** birds. ____________________

____

5. It's a **queer** thing. ____________________

____

6. Mr. Popper put down his book … and moved **hastily** to the radio. ____________________

____

7. from the South Pole, a **faint** voice floated out into the Popper living room. __________

____

Comprehension Questions

1. What impresses Mr. Popper most about the Drake Expedition? ______________________

____

____

2. What words does Mr. Popper use to describe penguins to Mrs. Popper? ______________

____

____

3. Explain how the penguins catch shrimp. ______________________________

____

____

4. Why is Mr. Popper excited about September 29th? ______________________

____

____

5. What unexpected event happens that day? ______________________

____

____

Activity

Complete the following:

- Find an old National Geographic magazine and read about exotic places.
- Make a picture collage of exotic places you would like to visit. Locate them on a map or globe.
- Learn about the differences between the North and South Poles.
- Research the Poles and penguins. Write a paragraph detailing a penguin's natural habitat and daily routines.

Pronounce & Spell

curiosity	wrappings	heart	package
receipt	succeeded	circles	gentleman

Vocabulary

Write the meaning of each bold word or phrase.

1. "Very well, my love," said Mr. Popper **meekly** ______________________________

____

2. It was an **expressman** with the largest box Mr. Popper had ever seen. ____________

____

3. part of the packing, which was a layer of **dry ice** ____________________________

____

4. His hands were trembling so that he could **scarcely** lift off the last of the wrappings. ____

____

5. this time it held out its flippers and jumped over the packing **debris**. ______________

____

6. Down the hall it went and into the bedrooms, with its strange, **pompous** little strut. _____

____

7. the **inquisitive** bird kept reaching over and trying to bite the faucets ______________

____

Comprehension Questions

1. Describe the package that is delivered to Mr. Popper. ________________________________

____

____

2. What emerges from the box? ____

____

3. Describe the gift in detail. ____

____

____

____

4. Why is the bathroom so attractive to the guest? ____________________________

____

____

5. Why does Mr. Popper fill the bathtub? ______________________________________

____

____

6. How does the guest get his name? ____

____

____

Activity

Complete the following:

- Research the historical significance of the name Captain Cook.
- Track the real Captain Cook's route on a map or globe.
- Write a vivid description of the package that Mr. Popper received. Be sure to appeal to each of the five senses. Consider how you want your reader to respond to your description. Do you want him to be scared of the box? Excited about the box? Curious about it? Try to appeal to your reader's emotion when describing the package.

Pronounce & Spell

famous	ceiling	upholstered	scientific
biting	refrigerator	squatted	naughty

Vocabulary

Write the meaning of each bold word or phrase.

1. who lived about the time of the **American Revolution**. ______________________________

   ____

2. I think Captain Cook would be a very **suitable** name ______________________________

   ____

3. "Stop him, Papa!" screamed Mrs. Popper, **retreating** into the hallway __________________

   ____

4. "Gork?" he inquired … looking at her **pleadingly** with his right eye. __________________

   ____

5. Then he walked **solemnly** around the table … inspecting everything. __________________

   ____

6. he stood still, very **erect**, raised his beak to point at the ceiling, and make a loud, almost purring sound. ____

   ____

7. Then he left the door **ajar** so that the penguin would have plenty of fresh air ____________

   ____

Comprehension Questions

1. Why does Mr. Popper name his penguin Captain Cook? ______________________________

2. How does Captain Cook get in trouble with Mrs. Popper? ______________________________

3. Describe Captain Cook's sleeping quarters. ______________________________

4. Why does Mrs. Popper believe the penguin will be a good example for the children? ______________________________

5. List several things Mr. Popper does to make Captain Cook more comfortable in his new home. ______________________________

Activity

Complete the following:

- Research the American Revolution.
- Write a list of the major events of the war.
- Draw a picture of Captain Cook in his new home.

Pronounce & Spell

license	violent	noises	pieces
trouble	examined	remodeled	policeman

Vocabulary

Write the meaning of each bold word or phrase.

1. Mister, you don't need no **ventilating** holes in that there door. ____________________

   ____

2. It's my **icebox**, and I want some holes **bored** in the door. a)____________________

   b)____

3. He didn't want to discuss Captain Cook with this **unsympathetic** service man __________

   ____

4. "Don't get funny," said Mr. Popper **indignantly**. ____________________

   ____

5. the service man had no **intention** of putting on an inside handle. ____________________

   ____

6. That's the first **sensible** thing you've said yet. ____________________

   ____

7. Mr. Popper **promptly** put Captain Cook back inside ____________________

   ____

Comprehension Questions

1. The first sentence on page 31 says, "The next day was quite eventful." Explain why. ______

2. Why does the serviceman think Mr. Popper is "not quite right"? ______

3. How does Mr. Popper finally get the serviceman to put a handle on the inside of the door?

4. What does Captain Cook think of his new entrance to his quarters? ______

5. Why do you think the policeman visits the Popper home? ______

Activity

Complete the following:

- Think of other places in a home or neighborhood that a penguin might like to live.
- Write a list of other types of homes for a penguin. Rank them from most desirable to least desirable for a penguin.
- Re-tell the exciting events of the day in a five-sentence paragraph. Start by writing five sentences, using the cue words **first**, **second**, **third**, **next**, and **finally** to start your sentences. Improve each sentence and then combine them to form a paragraph. Be sure to indent the first sentence of your paragraph and punctuate every sentence correctly.

Pronounce & Spell

arrest	sergeant	laugh	scratch
leash	loose	puzzled	telephone

Vocabulary

Write the meaning of each bold word or phrase.

1. "Gook," said Captain Cook walking with **dignity** ______________________

____

2. I don't know what the **municipal ordinance** about penguins is ______________________

____

3. This went on for **considerable** time. ______________________

____

4. And please try to speak a little more **distinctly** ______________________

____

5. "Then listen," roared Mr. Popper, now completely **outraged**. ______________________

____

6. Our own Mr. Treadbottom of the **Bureau** of Navigation of Lakes, Rivers, Ponds, and Streams, has just come in. ______________________

____

Comprehension Questions

1. Why doesn't the policeman come inside the Poppers' house? ________________________________

____

____

2. How does the conversation with the policeman end? ________________________________

____

____

3. What does Captain Cook do to make the phone call more difficult for Mr. Popper? ________

____

____

4. Describe two people Mr. Popper talks to before he finally hangs up the telephone. ________

____

____

____

5. Does Mr. Popper resolve his problem with the people at City Hall? ________________________

____

____

Activity

Complete the following:

- Look up the ordinances for the place where you live. Note any interesting rules.
- Are there any rules related to animals for your neighborhood, town, city, or county?
- Write a paragraph to summarize Mr. Popper's phone call to City Hall. Use interesting details about each person Mr. Popper spoke with, and explain the result of each conversation. Be sure to include Mr. Popper's reactions.

Pronounce & Spell

frequently	furniture	excellent	splendid
prowled	straightening	thoroughness	occurred

Vocabulary

Write the meaning of each bold word or phrase.

1. Very **reluctantly**, Janie and Bill had to leave Captain Cook and go to school. ___________

____

2. Mrs. Popper was busy in the kitchen, rather **belatedly** doing the breakfast dishes ________

____

3. she **dimly** realized that the penguin was going in and out the refrigerator pretty frequently

____

4. Meanwhile Mr. Popper had **abandoned** his telephoning and was now busy shaving ______

____

5. But the penguin … was by no means **idle**. ___________________________

____

6. with little **subdued** cries of curiosity, surprise, and pleasure. ___________________

____

7. Never again would Mrs. Popper have to **reproach** him for looking as wild as a lion. ______

____

Comprehension Questions

1. What is Captain Cook working on during the morning chores? ______________________

____

____

2. List some of the most interesting items in Captain Cook's nest. ______________________

____

____

____

3. What does Mr. Popper call Captain Cook's nest? ______________________

____

4. Describe how Mr. Popper looks when he takes Captain Cook out for a walk. ____________

____

____

____

5. Find out what these words and phrases mean:

   flannel trousers ______________________

   oxblood shoes ______________________

   cedar chest ______________________

   tailcoat ______________________

Activity

Complete the following:

- Write a list of every item Captain Cook included in his nest. How many items were there all together?
- Draw a picture of Captain Cook's nest.
- Research rookeries. Find out how penguins usually build them.
- List interesting facts about rookeries and penguins' nests on another piece of paper. Include the facts in a report.

Pronounce & Spell

protesting	investigate	exclaimed	exhibits
scene	groceries	believed	obediently

Vocabulary

Write the meaning of each bold word or phrase.

1. when he saw that protesting did him no good, he recovered his **customary** dignity ______

____

2. Mr. Popper put on his best Sunday **derby** ______________________

____

3. Heaven **preserve** us! ______________________________

____

4. These he **evidently** mistook for polar snow ______________________

____

5. for he began to peck at the window **vigorously**. ______________________

____

6. I'd think it was a **dodo**, only dodos are **extinct**. a)______________________

b)____

7. Spying the camera **tripod**, he walked over and examined it. ______________

____

8. At last, Captain Cook, standing still beside Mr. Popper, **consented** to pose. ________

____

Comprehension Questions

1. Describe how Mr. Popper conducts his walk with Captain Cook. ______________________

2. How does Mrs. Callahan react to seeing the penguins? ______________________

3. What two kinds of birds do the photographer and the cameraman guess Captain Cook might be? ______________________

4. How did they convince themselves otherwise? ______________________

5. Why do you think the reporter does not believe Mr. Popper when he explains how Captain Cook came to live with him? ______________________

Activity

Complete the following:

- Research pelicans and dodos.
- Compare and contrast penguins, pelicans, and dodos.
- Draw a picture of each bird.
- Write a paragraph on dodos or pelicans. Read it aloud to the class.

Identifying Quotations

Write the names of the characters who spoke each of the quotations listed below.

1. "Gork?" ______________________________

2. "Look, Papa. There's a policeman at the back door. Is he going to arrest you?" ______________________________

3. "Hey, pelican, turn around and see the pretty birdie." ______________________________

4. "Well, dear me, I never thought we would have a penguin for a pet." ______________________________

5. "And look how his little black coat drags behind. It almost looks as if it were too big for him." ______________________________

6. "Not anteater. Antarctic. It was sent to me from the South Pole." ______________________________

7. "I'd think it was a dodo, only dodos are extinct." ______________________________

8. "Thanks for your nice letter about the pictures of our last expedition." ______________________________

9. "Take your South Pole goose away from me at once." ______________________________

10. "You call up the City Hall and ask them what the ruling about penguins is." ______________________________

Illustrating a Scene

In the box below, choose and illustrate a scene from what you have read so far. Use visual details so that anyone who looks at your drawing will be able to recognize the characters, setting, and action.

Pronounce & Spell

ledge	polite	plunge	reclining
delighted	quick	exercise	humble

Vocabulary

Write the meaning of each bold word or phrase.

1. Captain Cook found this **spectacle** very interesting ______________________________

____

2. The gentleman in the barber's chair, his face already white with **lather** ____________

____

3. Mr. Popper took Captain Cook in his arms, and **amid** cries … made his way out of the shop ____

____

4. "All right," said Mr. Popper, **panting** up the steps behind Captain Cook. ____________

____

5. Slowly but **unweariyingly**, Captain Cook lifted one pink foot after another from one step to the next ____

____

6. The driver … did not laugh at his **oddly assorted** passengers until he had been paid. ____

____

7. he went to lie down, for he was quite **exhausted** from all the unusual exercise ________

____

Comprehension Questions

1. Why does the barber order Captain Cook out of his shop? ______________________

____

____

2. What is it "absolutely impossible" to keep Captain Cook from doing? ______________

____

____

3. What does Mr. Popper conclude is the reason Captain Cook loves the activity? ________

____

____

____

4. Why does tying one end of the clothesline to his wrist prove unwise for Mr. Popper? _____

____

____

5. Describe how Mr. Popper feels at the end of his walk with Captain Cook. __________

____

____

Activity

Complete the following:

- Have a class discussion about animals that live with your family.
- If you don't have any pets, imagine what kind of pet you would like to have.
- Draw a picture of your real or imaginary pet. Write its name on the picture.
- Write a letter to Mr. Popper offering new suggestions on how he might take Captain Cook on a walk. Explain why you think your method will work.

Pronounce & Spell

ceased	neighbors	opinion	marbles
address	temperature	aquarium	sympathetic

Vocabulary

Write the meaning of each bold word or phrase.

1. Next day the picture of Mr. Popper and Captain Cook appeared in the Stillwater Morning **Chronicle** ______________________________

____

2. the photograph, **in rotogravure**, could be seen in the Sunday edition ______________________________

____

3. would sit most of the day, **sulking**, in the refrigerator. ______________________________

____

4. it was something worse than mopiness that **ailed** Captain Cook. ______________________________

____

5. I think you had better call the **veterinary doctor**. ______________________________

____

6. an Antarctic penguin can't **thrive** in Stillwater ______________________________

____

7. He slept all day now in a heavy **stupor** ______________________________

____

Comprehension Questions

1. How do the Poppers know something is wrong with Captain Cook? ________________

____

____

____

2. What does the doctor prescribe for the sick penguin? ________________

____

____

3. Why does he think the case is hopeless? ________________

____

____

4. As a last resort, what does Mr. Popper do to help Captain Cook? ________________

____

____

5. What is the grand result of Mr. Popper's effort? ________________

____

____

Activity

Complete the following:

- Find out if there are penguins at the zoo in your city. Visit them if you are able.
- Write a letter to a veterinarian or a zoo to inquire about the penguins there. Ask the zookeeper to share any information available on how to care for a penguin. Share with your class any response you receive.

Pronounce & Spell

friendship	slippery	occupied	checker
comfortable	enough	healthy	weather

Vocabulary

Write the meaning of each bold word or phrase.

1. he's trying to show that he's **grateful** to us for getting him Greta ____________________

   ____

2. **squirming** around in her nest, she turned her back to Mr. Popper. ____________________

   ____

3. there were large **drifts** of snow all over the house. ____________________

   ____

4. Both Greta and Captain Cook were **tremendously** pleased with all that ice. ____________

   ____

5. But Captain Cook and Greta are both fat and **sleek**. ____________________

   ____

6. the children have never been so **rosy**. ____________________

   ____

Comprehension Questions

1. What does Captain Cook do to show his appreciation to Mr. Popper? ________________

2. How do the Poppers mark Captain Cook and Greta to tell them apart? ________________

3. What worries Mrs. Popper about Captain Cook's and Greta's living space? ________________

4. List some things the Poppers do to accommodate the penguins. ________________

5. Describe how the floor is made into an ice rink. ________________

Activity

Complete the following:

- What other methods could you use to identify the penguins in a helpful, yet unharmful way?
- Draw a picture of the Poppers' house with the blizzard inside.
- Write a paragraph describing the Poppers' house with the blizzard inside. Detail the way the house looked and how the Poppers reacted to the wintery weather. Use strong adjectives and clear descriptions. Include adverbs to make your verbs more interesting.

Pronounce & Spell

relief	castle	hatch	appeared
expensive	electric	parade	fantastic

Vocabulary

Write the meaning of each bold word or phrase.

1. So the next day Mr. Popper called an **engineer** and had a large freezing plant installed ___

____

2. Mr. Popper promised to pay … and the man let him have everything on **credit**. _______________

____

3. They were fuzzy, **droll** little creatures who grew at a tremendous rate. _______________

____

4. two of them … began to **spar** at each other with their flippers _______________

____

5. Louisa seemed especially fond of leading these **marching drills**. _______________

____

6. he **dreaded** to think of the time when spring would come _______________

____

Comprehension Questions

1. How many eggs do penguins usually lay per season? ______

2. How many eggs does Greta lay in total, and how frequently does an egg appear? ______

3. What problem do the eggs create? ______

4. How does Mr. Popper resolve the problem? ______

5. Name the penguin children. ______

6. Describe the eating habits of the penguins. ______

Activity

Complete the following:

- List each of the children's names. Try to discover why Mr. Popper chose each name. Remember Mr. Popper's interests and hobbies.
- Write a sentence explaining the historical significance of each of the young penguins' names.

Pronounce & Spell

vacation	costumes	theaters	twelve
balanced	especially	soldiers	piano

Vocabulary

Write the meaning of each bold word or phrase.

1. Well, I don't **suppose** I really could enjoy eating them. ______________________________

____

2. you have heard of **trained** seals, acting in theaters ______________________________

____

3. climb up steps and **toboggan** down. ______________________________

____

4. Janie and Bill would drag out into the middle of the ice two **portable** stepladders ________

____

5. Mrs. Popper would play a pretty, **descriptive** piece called "By the Brook." ____________

____

6. It was cold in the **cellar**, of course ______________________________

____

Comprehension Questions

1. What new worry does Mrs. Popper have? ______________________________

2. What suggestions does Mrs. Popper have for fixing the problem? ______________________________

3. What is Mr. Popper's suggestion? ______________________________

4. What do the Poppers do to implement Mr. Popper's plan? ______________________________

5. Describe the penguins' acts. ______________________________

Activity

Complete the following:

- Listen to Schubert's "Military March" and Franz Lehár's "Merry Widow Waltz," and describe the songs using strong adjectives. Do you think these were good musical selections for the acts the penguins performed?
- Learn about Schubert, the composer of the "Military March."
- Write a detailed description of your favorite trick that the penguins performed. Explain it clearly for someone who has not read this book.

Pronounce & Spell

astonished	double	refused	fashion
conference	passengers	chorus	ballet

Vocabulary

Write the meaning of each bold word or phrase.

1. before the astonished driver could **protest**, they had all climbed on and the bus was on its way. ______________________________

   ____

2. Where do you think you're going with that **exhibit**? ______________________________

   ____

3. "Fair enough," said Mr. Popper, who wanted to ask for **transfers** in that case ___________

   ____

4. It took Mr. Popper quite a while to open the windows, which were stuck **fast**. ___________

   ____

5. "Hello," said the theater manager, as the Poppers and the penguins **trooped** past him. ___

   ____

6. That sounds too much like **chorus girls** or ballet dancers ______________________________

   ____

Comprehension Questions

1. Describe the Poppers' trip to the theater.

2. Why does the family get kicked off the bus?

3. What name does Mr. Popper want to call the group of penguins?

4. What name does Mr. Greenbaum suggest for the group?

5. Why does Mr. Popper decline?

Activity

Complete the following:

- Draw a picture of the penguins walking to the bus stop. Label each person or penguin.
- Draw a poster advertising Popper's Performing Penguins.
- Write an advertisement for Popper's Performing Penguins. Explain why someone would want to see the penguins' performance, using carefully chosen words. Remember, in an advertisement you have a very limited opportunity to make your point—every word must be well chosen!

Studying Characters

Write the name of each listed character on the line above that character's description.
Each name can be used only one time.

Characters	Descriptions
Mr. Popper	______ saved Captain Cook
Mrs. Popper	______ dreams about far-away places
Janie	______ the first penguin
Captain Cook	______ owns many theaters
Mr. Greenbaum	______ the Poppers' son
Admiral Drake	______ worries about money in winter
Greta	______ South Pole explorer
Bill	______ the Poppers' daughter

Illustrating a Scene

In the box below, choose and illustrate a scene from what you have read so far. Use visual details so that anyone who looks at your drawing will be able to recognize the characters, setting, and action.

Pronounce & Spell

manager	applauded	rehearse	audiences
formation	immediately	discipline	congratulate

Vocabulary

Write the meaning of each bold word or phrase.

1. with your kind **indulgence** we are going to try out a little **novelty** number tonight. a)______ ____________________ b) ____________________

2. Owing to **unforeseen circumstances**, the Marvelous Marcos are unable to appear ______ ____________________

3. In a **dignified** way the Poppers and the penguins walked out on the stage… ____________ ____________________

4. wheeling and changing their **formations** with great **precision** a) ____________________ ____________________ b) ____________________

5. Columbus then counted ten over the **prostrate** Nelson ____________________ ____________________

6. you've got something absolutely **unique** in those birds. Your act is a **sensation**. a) ______ ____________________ b)____________________

7. the way you helped out my friend … shows that you're real **troupers** ____________________ ____________________ ____________________

Comprehension Questions

1. How do the penguins get the chance to perform for a live audience? ____________________
____
____

2. Describe the audience's reaction to the first act. ____________________
____
____

3. Who wins the penguin fight? ____________________
____

4. What does Mr. Greenbaum think of the performance? ____________________
____
____

5. Detail the offer that is made to the Poppers. ____________________
____
____
____

6. What lesson does the manager want the penguins to teach the ushers? ____________
____
____

Activity

Complete the following:

- List the ten stops in the U.S. you would make if you were able to map the penguins' tours.
- On a U.S. map, plot your "wish trip" in the most efficient way, marking the stops in the order you would make them (Stop #1, 2, 3, etc.).
- Explain your reasons for choosing the ten stops you would make on the penguins' tour.

Pronounce & Spell

temptation	lantern	observation	accident
nervous	eager	interfered	conductor

Vocabulary

Write the meaning of each bold word or phrase.

1. she was much too good a housekeeper to leave everything at **sixes and sevens** ________

____

2. Mr. Popper should ride in the **baggage** car ________________________

____

3. In the sleeping cars … the porter was already making up some of the **berths** ________

____

4. There were a dozen happy Orks from a dozen **ecstatic** beaks. ________________

____

5. A gentleman wearing a **clergyman's collar** suggested opening a window ________

____

6. you must remember, my love, that travel is very **broadening**. ________________

____

7. From the start the penguins were a **riotous** success. ________________

____

Comprehension Questions

1. What do the Poppers do with their first week's advance pay? ____________________

____

2. What happens on the way to the station? How are the Poppers partly responsible? ______

____

____

____

3. How do the penguins misbehave on the train? ____________________

____

____

4. How do audiences respond to the penguins' performances? ____________________

____

____

____

5. Describe the scene with the penguins and the tightrope walker, Monsieur Duval. ________

____

____

____

____

Activity

Complete the following:

- Read about trains. What were they like for travel? What were popular train routes in the U.S.? What happened to the railroad lines?
- Why do most people not travel by train anymore? Have you ever taken a trip on a passenger train?
- When did this story take place? Write at least five sentences describing the clues that let you know the story did not take place in the present time and that might support your guess.

Pronounce & Spell

orchestra	opportunities	guilty	musicians
occasionally	mischief	brief	irritable

Vocabulary

Write the meaning of each bold word or phrase.

1. in another minute the audience was **shrieking** with laughter ____________________

 ____

2. That stopped the singing entirely except for one high, **shrill** note ____________________

 ____

3. Now and then a **startled** hotelkeeper would object to having the birds ______________

 ____

4. Mr. Popper, who never liked to be a **nuisance** to anyone, always took taxis ____________

 ____

5. Mr. Popper had written a **testimonial** ______________________________

 ____

6. Mr. Popper had to have the ice brought up to his rooms in **thousand-pound cakes**. _____

 ____

Comprehension Questions

1. Why did other performers not like to be scheduled with the penguins? ________________

____

____

2. What do the penguins do to disrupt the opera singer's performance? ________________

____

____

3. What do the penguins think about performing and traveling? ________________

____

____

4. Are the Poppers making money traveling? Explain why or why not. ________________

____

____

____

____

5. How do they earn extra income? ________________

____

____

Activity

Complete the following:

- List the cities the Poppers will visit on their tour. Spell each correctly and name the state it is in.
- Map the Poppers' course on a map. Compare it to your "wish trip."
- What do you know about each city they will visit?
- Think of a product that you really like or appreciate. Write a testimonial for it, trying to persuade others to use it or buy it.

Pronounce & Spell

canyons	mustaches	seals	bathed
business	traffic	disturber	square

Vocabulary

Write the meaning of each bold word or phrase.

1. "Yes sir," said the driver, **threading** his way in and out the traffic ____________________

   ____

2. In the wings stood a large **burly**, red-faced man. ______________________________

   ____

3. From the stage could be heard the **hoarse** barks of the seals ____________________

   ____

4. the audience was in an **uproar**, and the curtain was quickly rung down. ____________

   ____

5. they were a little **vexed** to find that there was no fire at all. ____________________

   ____

6. I have a **warrant** for his arrest. ____

   ____

Comprehension Questions

1. What does Mr. Popper think about when he sees the penguins on the roof?

2. What causes Mr. Popper to make his great mistake?

3. Who else is performing at the Regal Theater? Why is this a potential problem?

4. How do the policemen and the firemen get involved in the action? What are the teams?

5. What do the Poppers find when they go to check on the penguins and the seals?

Activity

Complete the following:

- Why do you think seals are often used in circus acts?
- Draw a picture of the conflict between the seals and the penguins.
- Research seals. Write a paragraph describing their habitat and daily activities. Read your paragraph to your class.

Pronounce & Spell

reception	patience	Hollywood	salary
anxious	apparent	decision	establishing

Vocabulary

Write the meaning of each bold word or phrase.

1. None of his **pleas** could move the desk sergeant. ______________________

____

2. I'm going to give you all a nice quiet cell—unless you **furnish** bail. ____________

____

3. Even the younger birds sat all day in **dismal** silence ______________________

____

4. Mr. Greenbaum would probably turn up … to see about **renewing** the contract. ______

____

5. About ten o'clock there was a sound of footsteps in the **corridor** ____________

____

6. Then, as his eyes became **accustomed** to the light, he looked again. __________

____

7. Here's Mr. Klein, who owns the **Colossal** Film Company. ______________________

____

Comprehension Questions

1. Why are Mr. Popper and the penguins thrown in jail? ______________________________

2. How much bail money has to be paid for their release? ______________________________

3. Who does Mr. Popper expect to bail him out of jail? Who comes to see Mr. Popper instead? ______________________________

4. What does Admiral Drake offer Mr. Popper? ______________________________

5. What does Mr. Klein offer Mr. Popper? ______________________________

Activity

Complete the following:

- Read about polar bears, where they live, and what they eat.
- Why would the government want to establish a breed of a particular animal?
- To compare two things means to find their similarities. To contrast means to find the differences. Write a paragraph that compares two things and contrasts two things about the North and South Poles.

Pronounce & Spell

advantages	announcement	visitors	government
climate	appreciate	reputation	familiar

Vocabulary

Write the meaning of each bold word or phrase.

1. she pointed these out, without trying to **influence** him. ______________________________

____

2. It was a pale and **haggard** Mr. Popper who was ready to announce his decision ________

____

3. Greta, too, had seen **vessels** of its kind. ______________________________

____

4. Bill and Janie … did not want to leave when it was time to draw up the **gangplank**. _______

____

5. the extraordinary penguins that were a real **contribution** to science. ________________

____

6. We're pulling **anchor** in a minute. ______________________________

____

Comprehension Questions

1. Which offer does Mr. Popper decide to accept? ____________________
2. How does this make him feel? ____________________
3. What preparations are made for the voyage? ____________________
4. How do the penguins react to the boat? ____________________
5. What exciting surprise does Mr. Popper receive as the boat is about to set sail? ____________________

Activity

Complete the following:

- Draw a picture of Mr. Popper departing for the Expedition with Admiral Drake.
- A book report always includes the book title, the author's name, and the copyright date. It also mentions the main characters, the setting, and the main events. In book reports, you should also share your opinion of the story. After you collect the necessary information, write a book report on *Mr. Popper's Penguins*.

Noticing Details

Look for answers to the following questions in *Mr. Popper's Penguins*.

1. How many baby penguins were born to Greta and Captain Cook? ____________________

____

2. What was Mr. Popper's real job? ____

3. What color were the penguins' feet? ____

____

4. How much money per week did the Poppers' penguins earn? ____________________

____

5. How many weeks of vacation did the Popper children take? ____________________

____

6. What was the result of the Associated Press getting the penguin story? ____________

____

7. What did Mrs. Popper refuse to remove while playing piano? ____________________

____

8. Which two penguins performed a boxing match in the act? ____________________

____

9. How much did Mr. Popper have to pay the refrigerator service man? ______________

____

10. In what month did Mr. Popper begin to dread the coming of Spring? ______________

____

11. What kept Captain Cook cool as he traveled from the South Pole? ______________

____

12. How many eggs do penguins usually lay in a season? ________________________

____

Illustrating a Scene

In the box below, choose and illustrate a scene from *Mr. Popper's Penguins*. Use visual details so that anyone who looks at your drawing will be able to recognize the characters, setting, and action.